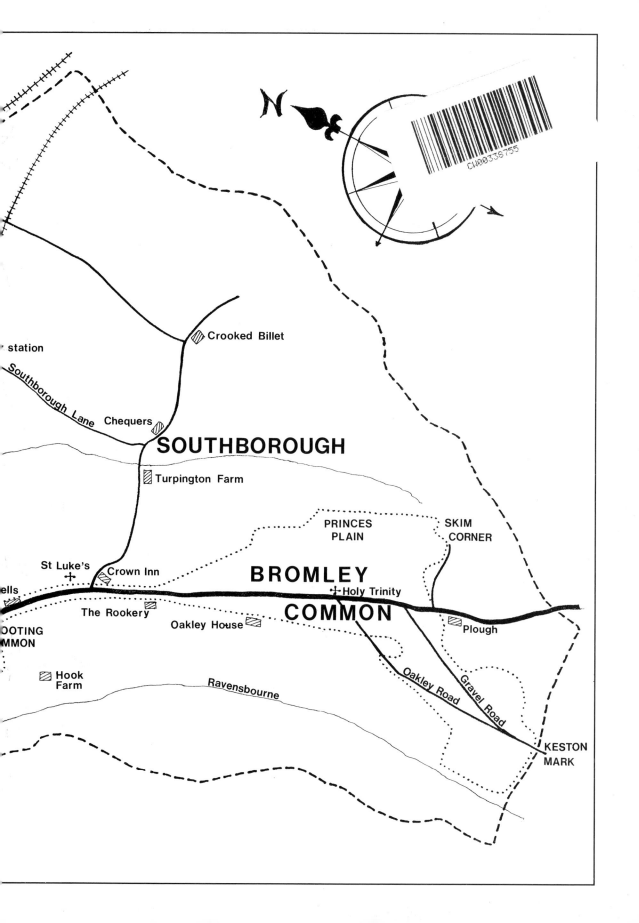

N

station

Southborough Lane Chequers

Crooked Billet

SOUTHBOROUGH

Turpington Farm

PRINCES
PLAIN

SKIM
CORNER

St Luke's Crown Inn

BROMLEY

ells

Holy Trinity

The Rookery

COMMON

Oakley House

Plough

OOTING
MMON

Hook
Farm

Ravensbourne

Oakley Road

Gravel Road

KESTON
MARK

BROMLEY
A Pictorial History

Widmore Road.

BROMLEY
A Pictorial History

edited by

Patricia E. Knowlden

for the

Bromley Borough Local History Society

Phillimore

1990

Published by
PHILLIMORE & CO. LTD.
Shopwyke Hall, Chichester, Sussex

ISBN 0 85033 753 4

Printed and bound in Great Britain by
BIDDLES LTD.
Guildford, Surrey

List of Illustrations

Illustration Acknowledgments

The editor is grateful to the following for permission to reproduce the illustrations: Bromley Bowling Club, 139, 140; Bromley Camera Club, 43-46; Bromley Cricket Club, 130, 132; Bromley Football Club, 41; Bromley High School, 95; Bromley Hockey Club, 133, 134; Bromley Leisure Services, 9, 10, 13, 14, 24, 36, 39, 40, 47, 50, 56-58, 64, 66, 72, 74, 81, 83, 85, 94, 96, 97, 105, 138, 141, 142, 146, 149, 150, 156, 159, 160; Christ Church, 157, 158; John Edwards, 152; Mrs. Kitty Eisele, 92; Holy Trinity Convent School, 136, 137; Geoffrey Knowlden, 102; Pat Last, 93; Bill Morton, 5, 11, 12, 17, 26, 28, 32-34, 37, 51, 53, 59, 61, 68-70, 75, 76, 80, 88, 98, 103, 111, 117, 125, 131, 143, 151; Doris Pullen, 4; Raglan Road School, 104; Leslie Stevens, 1, 3, 6, 21-23, 29, 31, 35, 42, 49, 52, 54, 65, 79, 82, 87, 101, 107, 123, 126, 127, 135, 153-155; St Mark's church, 89-91; St Mary's church, 147, 148; Valley Primary School, 7, 8; Harry Walden, 38; Philip Wilson, 48.

Acknowledgments

Firstly, to our very good friends the Staff of the Local Studies Room at Bromley Central Library for their unfailing help and co-operation, and for permission to reproduce a number of items from the collection of illustrations. To members of Bromley Borough Local History Society goes the credit for much of the text, especially to Len Smith for the section on Bromley Common; to Joyce Walker (Health); Jean Wilson (Education); Elaine Baker (Religion); Muriel Searle (Bromley Football Club); John Edwards (Transport); Alex Freeman, Local Studies Librarian (Local Government); Brenda Innes (New Bromley); Michael Rawcliffe (Housing Development); Geoffrey Eames (Bromley Cricket and Hockey Clubs); Joy Maynard for permission to quote from a letter of Florence Nightingale, also Pat Last (Masons Hill and St Mark's); Ron Driver (Bromley Camera Club); and many other Bromley organisations for their help with relevant captions. We are grateful to Mary Konior and W.E. Fairhead for reading the text and to Sheila Pritchard for proof reading. Thanks are also due to Peter Francis and Geoffrey Knowlden for photographic copying.

Foreword

From being the home of a Bishop and medieval market town, Bromley or 'the place where the broom grows' has grown to a prosperous thriving London Borough.

I congratulate Messrs. Phillimore on publishing this wonderful collection of Victorian and Edwardian photographs which illustrate the growth of our town. Many of the buildings shown have now disappeared but thankfully many remain to give the town its character and remind us of our past.

We are still a market town with trade now concentrated in our vast shopping areas instead of our market. Government is still exercised from the old Bishop's Palace which now forms part of our Civic Centre. Bromley, the gateway to Kent and where the broom still grows.

TOM AINSBY

Mayor (1989-90),
London Borough of Bromley,
Mayor's Parlour,
The Old Palace,
Bromley.

Introduction

A prosperous and well-built town, the buildings continually increase. Its situation is pleasant and healthy and among its inhabitants are many opulent gentlemen's families which, together with the College and Bishop of Rochester's residence nearby and its frequent market, support it in a most flourishing condition.

Thus Kentish historian William Ireland described Bromley in 1828. Twenty years later *Bagshaw's Directory for Kent* quotes Ireland almost word for word – but puts the prosperity in the past, the markets discontinued and the town 'decayed'. At the time when photography was being invented Bromley was in the doldrums.

Much of this prosperity had been due to a Dr. Scott whose treatment for leg ulcers had drawn many affluent residents to the town. His retirement, in 1829, was followed not long afterwards by the loss of Bromley's lords of the manor; for nearly 1,000 years Bromley had belonged to the Bishops of Rochester who used the palace they built here as a staging post on the way to London and often as a residence. Having the bishops here was ever an economic benefit. It was they who, in 1205, established the market which over the centuries turned the country village into the commercial centre. A 17th-century bishop left money for Bromley College, and having its 20 genteel widows living in their midst as well as the household at the Palace itself gave a continuing boost to local tradesmen. The departure of the bishops, then, was much deplored – until the eventual arrival of a new landowner in the person of Mr. Coles Child, who set about revitalising the town.

Coles Child took his position as lord of the manor seriously, both insisting on his ancient dues when, for instance, property changed hands and also doing a great deal for the place, rescuing the market and – his most noticable contribution – replacing the old wooden market house with an imposing red-brick building. It is at this stage that Bromley's photographic record begins, with pictures of the Market Square before and after the great change. Although criticised by the more reactionary inhabitants for an over-powering appearance, the new Town Hall's larger size gave opportunities for a wide range of social activities. Space was allowed for a library and also for the police station; from here every evening around 10 p.m. emerged the night watch, oil hand-lamps at the ready, to patrol the Market Place and High Street, trying doors and shutters of each of the premises even though most of the proprietors lived 'over the shop'. Commercial, business and private premises were intermingled in the old town. Many of the buildings in the mid-19th century were still timber-framed (a few are today) although they were gradually being replaced by modern brick with slate roofs. There were still trees in Upper High Street and gardens off the Market Square.

The town still began, as it had for centuries, at Bromley College in the London Road. Even today the College is a peaceful island in its grounds, two cloistered quadrangles of red-brick houses with grassy lawns. Past the gates flows the main stream of traffic – which

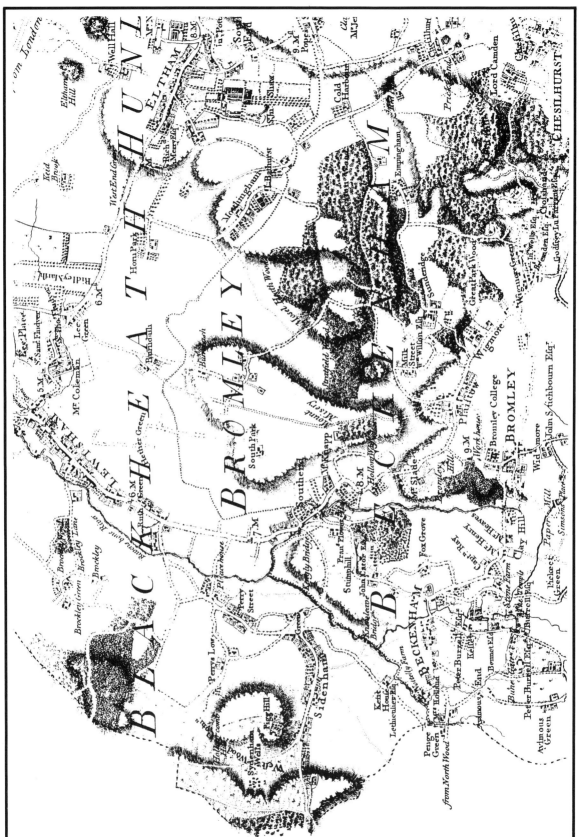

A Topographical Map of the county of Kent, 1769

in the 1800s consisted of farmers' wagons and carriers' carts, carriages of the gentry, and delivery vans. Only a few years earlier, the long-distance coaches had brought commotion to the principal inns several times a day. The High Street ran on past the turning to the parish church on the right, and the market place on the left. Another 200-300 yards along the shops ended, then the grounds of large houses stretched to the bottom of the hill. From there the road climbed through the hamlet of Masons Hill, home and workplace to carpenters, blacksmiths and other skilled artisans. At the top the country began again.

Bromley had four other ancient hamlets scattered among the fields besides many farms and a number of estates with country mansions, for successful merchants had for centuries made their homes a half-day's ride from London. It was the sale of one of these estates that sparked off Bromley's metamorphosis from market town to suburb. In 1841 Bickley Park came into the hands of receivers who divided the property for sale, and a large portion just north-east of the town was laid out in building plots. This came to be known as New Bromley. Then when Coles Child bought Bromley Palace and the bishops' estate he partially financed himself by selling some of the land for speculative building. The big houses down the hill went next and gracious lawns on the one side and a blackberry patch on the other disappeared under the Victorian villas of Elmfield Road and Ringers Road. During the 1860s, '70s and '80s Bromley spread ever further. The population, which had been 5,500 in 1861, nearly quadrupled in 30 years. And Bromley was now only 20 minutes journey time to the city of London – by train:

> Take the 9.15 morning train from Bromley for instance; for, being an express train very many season- and not a few day-ticket holders avail themselves of a train which professes to get to Cannon Street and sometimes really does do it, in 20 minutes ...

The coming of the railways to all parts of England ended the time-honoured system of travelling by horse-drawn public coaches. Following the arrival of the railway in Bromley in 1858, all the long-distance coaches in the area faded away by the 1880s. The first railway station at the bottom of the High Street, on a site previously occupied by the Charity Schools, was simply called Bromley. There was a regular service to Charing Cross; and from there trains called at Waterloo Junction and Cannon Street before reversing to call at London Bridge, and on down the line to Beckenham Junction, Shortlands, then Bromley, to terminate at Bickley. These trains were provided by the South Eastern Railway. Two years later the London Chatham and Dover Company began to run trains through Bromley via St Mary Cray to Victoria, and opened their new route through to Farringdon Street in 1866. Horse buses were scheduled to meet four up and four down trains daily and proceeded to Keston, calling at the *Crown Inn* on Bromley Common on the way. On weekdays three more buses operated by William Lownds, the publican of the *White Hart*, went to Keston via Hayes. At the *Beech Tree* in London Road, F. Austen advertised 'cabs to and from all stations', and all sorts of horse-drawn vehicles were available from William Withycombe at the *Royal Oak* in Farwig, among others. The Catford Loop Line was opened in 1892.

The other station now in Bromley, which became Bromley North, was opened on New Year's Day 1878 by the Bromley Direct Company and the next year was absorbed by the South Eastern Railway. While Bromley North proved useful to travellers, the building has been described as 'a construction which can only be called an apology for a station hastily thrown together' – a clap-board building which was not replaced until 1926. After years of feuding rivalry, in 1899 the South Eastern and the London Chatham and Dover Railways decided to form a working partnership, which would be known as the South Eastern and Chatham until the grouping of 1923. The combination of easy travelling with land available for development induced a population growth that strained the existing public services beyond their limits. The Local Boards, whose task it was to provide these things, found it hard to know what to do for the best.

Under the terms of the Local Government Act of 1858, the administration of the general business of the town passed from the vestry to the Local Board, first elected in 1867. This board fulfilled the role of local government authority until it, too, was superseded by the Urban District Council under the Act of 1894. E.L.S. Horsburgh, in his history of Bromley published in 1929, remarks about this era of local government:

> The history of this period is a tumultuous one for, from the first, it seemed to be impossible for the Board to do anything right ... it failed to secure either the confidence or the affection of the public.

Strong words indeed, but were these criticisms justified? Within local government at this time the main branches were the administration of the poor laws and of public health, the principal authorities being the town council or Local Board, the Sanitary Board and the Board of Guardians. However, one earnest and intelligent reformer described the system as 'a chaos of areas, a chaos of franchises, a chaos of authorities and a chaos of rates'. Old and new members of the growing community together formed Bromley's Local Board – and others formed an opposition which kept them on their toes. Sometimes the roles were reversed, which made things lively and progressive. Besides the vexed problem of drains, there was the problem of providing schools; more churches had to be built and there was a growing need for a library and similar facilities.

The Local Board was a very political body. Initially it included a gentry element which was soon ousted by the traders, who were then accused of similar inadequacies and lampooned in the local press: 'Tell me not in mournful number ... that our Local Board is dead ... Oh dear no, they only slumber ... wake them not, they're best in bed!'

The aspect of Bromley's corporate planning that was the subject of most altercation at the time was the drainage of the town, the removal both of surface rain-water and of other less pleasant liquid wastes. Even the more genteel residences suffered from odours and stenches as the older houses were built with cesspools and water closets were untrapped; this, at a time when bad smells were actually thought to cause diseases, must have been worrying. New Bromley, being the recent extension of the town, was in the forefront of the debate. At Wharton Terrace, for instance, where 16 cottages shared one 13-ft. deep well only 12ft. away from a cesspool, drainage became an urgent problem. No doubt sanitation in the High Street area and the outlying farming hamlets was primitive – earth closets or cesspools for the few indoor W.C.s. But gradually, spurred on by criticism – especially from Charles Gedney's *Bromley Telegraph*, dubbed *The Scorpion* – pavements were laid, the streets lit and in 1878 they even began to solve the drainage problem by the creation of the West Kent Main Sewerage Board. Eventually the Board 'which drains our pockets but not the town' did succeed and Arthur Codd, the Medical Officer of Health, was able to report in 1890 that 'the sanitary requirements have received that attention which is so necessary during the growth of a new district, and which if maintained in these days of demand for sanitation, must gain the town increasing popularity and prosperity'.

New roads were also being laid and had to be made up, such as that linking West Street to College Road, so opening up the way to Plaistow. Other amenities were gradually provided. In May 1890, for instance, the Grand Hall was opened in the High Street, complete with swimming pool in the basement. But 'enterprise is dead in Bromley', grumbled a *Bromley Record* correspondent, 'or we would have had baths before now'. What he said when they had to close again because the back wall bulged when swimmers dived in is not recorded. Nevertheless, even Horsburgh admits that much was accomplished and the Local Board 'could look back upon its career with satisfaction and complacency'.

Bromley Charity Schools had been established in 1717 in a disused gravel pit at the foot of Masons Hill to teach the children of 'the poorer sort' reading and writing and such other things as were useful and suitable to their condition and capacity! When this became a National School in 1814 the building was enlarged to cope with growing numbers, but 40 years later even this was inadequate and new Parish Schools were built in the fields east of Bromley College. By 1870 there were four National (Church) Schools providing education for working class children in the district: Bromley Parish School; Plaistow National School opened in 1863; Bromley Common National School in 1864; and an infants' school in Palace Road in New Bromley. More National Schools were built after 1870. St Mark's School was intended to incorporate the infants from Palace Road and opened at Masons Hill in 1872. Bickley and Widmore National School was built the following year. In 1880 Mr. and Mrs. Edward Scott provided an elementary school for the children on the Sundridge Park estate. For children in the Chatterton Road district a temporary 'iron' building was erected on the south side of Pope Road which the Education Department refused to recognise. So in 1882 a massive effort was made to raise money to build a permanent school. Over £1,300 was promised and in July 1883 the Addison Road School for 244 children opened. Still the Education Department maintained that a further 600 places were necessary. Reluctantly the managers of the National Schools concluded that they were unable 'to take any steps towards supplying the deficiency'.

The time had come for elections to be held for a school board so these were fixed for 5 May 1888. 'The town has almost been turned topsy-turvey and not even at county elections can the oldest inhabitants remember so much disputation', reported the *District Times*. The main controversy was over the clause in the 1870 Act which stated that religious teaching in the Board Schools was to be non-denominational. The Church of England was not only determined to maintain its religious teachings in the Church Schools but also keen to influence what might happen in the new ones. It was, however, the three independent candidates who headed the poll when results were declared. Charles Gedney of the *Bromley Telegraph*, and a man of strong views, came top. Second was John Heelas Hall, who being a Wesleyan stood apart from the others. Next was Miss Mary Louise Heppel, headmistress of Bromley High School, who had been persuaded to stand by several ratepayers who felt that a board which was to control the education of both boys and girls must have a lady amongst its members. In the event, her election provided much-needed expertise on the board and did not harm the Anglicans. By June that year a census had been carried out showing that there was a deficiency of 1,293 places, and eventually it was agreed to provide further schools in the Shortlands, Bromley Common and Masons Hill areas.

For the more affluent members of the community a number of preparatory schools existed as well as at least three 'Middle Class Schools'. Until 1880 Bromley tradesmen sent their sons to Morley's Academy in the High Street. When Morley retired, John Gibson opened a new school which became the well-respected Quernmore; and there were others not so long lived. Smaller 'dame' schools came and went, such as Mrs. Knott's in South Street, where H.G. Wells was sent as a small boy.

Matters of health were tackled early as the result of an epidemic of cholera in 1831 when the streets of Bromley were defiled by pools of foul water and heaps of decomposing refuse; a Board of Health was set up to deal with sanitation and the condition of streets and houses. The first Medical Officer of Health was appointed in 1875, followed the next year by an Inspector of Nuisances. When Dr. Codd became M.O.H. in 1888 he was able to conclude his first report by saying that 'the general health of Bromley is extremely good', attributing this to its site, affluence and the effects of sanitary improvements and precautionary measures. Accommodation was featured in his report and he was concerned about the condition of some of the cottages, notably at New Bromley and Farwig where the poorest lived, and in Nicol Lane at Plaistow, where four cottages were condemned. The small houses intended for working people to rent were usually put up as investments by those of their own class who had been successful in earning enough money, for example Sinclair's Cottages which are still standing today. These had to be built cheaply and were crowded onto small sites as their builders did not have a lot to invest and the people for whom they were intended could not pay high rents. In the 1890s it was decided to make house-to-house inspections of cottage properties, and by 1904 the death rate was well down and most diseases abated. Another M.O.H. reporting on children attending the schools stated that many were developing headaches, but this was thought to be not from illness, rather from eye strain and excessive studying. The regular inspection of bake-houses, slaughter-houses and lodging-houses helped reduce the incidence of disease, as did tighter controls over the market, dairies and cowsheds. Under the Food and Drugs Act, 55 samples were purchased and submitted for analysis, with the result that many commodities, especially milk, were found to be more or less adulterated, and more than one offender was prosecuted.

Before 1869 patients needing in-hospital treatment could only hope to be accepted into the infirmary ward at the Union Workhouse at Farnborough or the isolation hospital at Skim Corner. That year the cottage hospital movement reached Bromley, when the editor of the *Bromley Record* drew the attention of his readers to an advertisement in his March edition 'from which they will see that an effort is being made to estabish a cottage hospital for the benefit of Bromley and the surrounding districts'. By May two small cottages had been purchased in Pieter's Lane (now Cromwell Avenue) and a six-bed hospital made ready for patients. A homeopathic hospital opened in 1889 and a 'fructarian' hospital (Lady Margaret's) of 16 beds in 1903, which grew to 40 by 1916. By that time the cottage hospital had been considerably enlarged, so within a matter of some 50 years the town was gradually supplied with adequate hospital care.

The church of St Peter and St Paul had served the parish for more than seven centuries when, in 1865, the Reverend Arthur Hellicar succeeded to the benefice. In his opinion a chancel was needed to bring the church into harmony with what he called 'the improved tone of church feelings'. So after much debate a committee was formed, funds were raised, and the chancel built in the Gothic style at a cost of £2,640, and consecrated in December 1884. On Sunday mornings the beadle stood at the lych gate in a long braided frock coat with gilt buttons, white choker and gold braided hat, carrying a tall staff of office surmounted by a gilded crown. This was Henry Checkley, who was also the last Victorian town crier of Bromley. The church dealt with social as well as spiritual needs. At the harvest festival in 1881 a visiting preacher reminded the congregation of recent misfortunes around the world: the year had not produced a bountiful harvest and he strongly deprecated the argument of some that, because it was not as good as it might have been, they should offer no thanks for it – a reminder of Bromley's rural character only about 100 years ago.

To serve the isolated area of Bromley Common, Holy Trinity church was built in 1841. By 1865 the religious worship of the Bickley area was centred around St George's and that of the northern part of Bromley around St Mary's at Plaistow. Here Major Clement Satterthwaite resided at Spring Hill, a dignified figure who took his seat in St Mary's every Sunday. He and his wife were prominent in all good works in the parish. In 1882, 400 children enjoyed their annual treat in his fields; a short service was followed by a march, with flags. Lunch, sports, cricket, and pony rides ensued. At 5 p.m. the children were summoned to a lavish tea. An observer noted that 'five balloons went up at 5.30 and much amusement was caused by an entirely new shape balloon which turned out to be none other than our old friend Jumbo'.

In the last quarter of the century Bromley was growing fast and still more churches were required so St John the Evangelist was opened in Park Road in 1871, Christ Church in Highland Road in 1887, St Mark's near Bromley South station ten years later, and St Luke's on Bromley Common in 1890. Roman Catholics in Bromley were served only by St Mary's at Chislehurst until 1886. Nonconformity did not make its appearance locally until the end of the 18th century, when a small chapel was opened off the Market Square for the Countess of Huntingdon's 'Connexion'. Later a larger chapel was built in Widmore Road which over the years developed a Congregational character. John Wesley himself preached at Widmore in 1772 and in the early 19th century a Wesleyan chapel was built off the Upper High Street; a new, larger, church in the Lower High Street opened for worship in 1876. The Baptists met at their chapel on the corner of Park and Tweedy Roads. Plymouth Brethren had a hall in Freelands Grove. The Salvation Army had barracks at Masons Hill from 1886 and there were numerous other small mission halls. Despite all these choices of church and chapel, when Mr. Matthew Hodder came to live in Bromley in 1865 he felt that the district lacked opportunity for religious worship (Mr. Hodder was founder of Hodder and Stoughton and at that time published many nonconformist religious books). So, for 37 years he led undenominational services in Great Elms Road. He strove to improve the lives of all local people through various institutions, and at his funeral people of all religious beliefs gathered to show their respect for a man who had so unselfishly devoted his life to the welfare of others – an early flowering of today's ecumenical spirit.

Every year the Congregational church provided Christmas dinners for 130 poor families in the parish. Every year Charles Gedney, the fiery editor of the *Bromley Telegraph*, spent his Christmas at the Union workhouse – that grim grey house as he called it – having already helped to organise the festivities. That the less fortunate were remembered at other times is evident from the local newspaper accounts. The longest running charity was arguably that of the Parish School, for in 1814 it was decided that their funds should be used for clothing 30 poor children: 'Both my sister and myself wore the awful clothing of the Charity Brats', recalled an ex-pupil! Bromley Philanthropic Friendly Society was established early in the grim 1840s. For the annual subscription of one shilling, members were entitled to nominate deserving cases for relief of coals or food, funds being raised by concerts and public lectures (the school fund was financed mainly by a prestigious yearly Charity Sermon). The Bromley Charitable Society, which did much useful work such as providing a good dinner for poor children two or three times a week, was founded in 1885. A saddler named John Lascoe left £2,880 in 1850 for a 'Decayed Tradesmen's

Charity Fund' and three years afterwards his sister bequeathed £150 to benefit four tradesmen's widows.

In the climate of the day it was expected that the citizens would be seen to support such charitable efforts, the Female Friendly Society, Church of England Working Men's Society, and the rest. Some of them made their names locally as philanthropists. Best loved was John Hall, a tallow-chandler, whose help for the needy so impoverished himself that in his old age his fellow-townsmen clubbed together to provide an annuity, which he enjoyed for ten years. He was best remembered for his efforts during the hard winter of 1878-9 when he collected £400 for those in want. He was rewarded by one of those doggerels in the local paper: 'Which is the *Great* Town Hall ... his Christian name is John ... he is the greatest Hall the Town possesses ... and kind philanthropy, we may be sure ... will well support him, while his Maker blesses ... his welcome mission to the humble poor'.

Leisure activities were of course by no means confined to charity concerts and penny readings and musical recitals. Most, however, were of rather an earnest persuasion, and the ancient fairs which had attracted boisterous crowds were suppressed in 1865. There was a tradition of horse-racing on Bromley Common, where steeple-chase meetings took place between 1864-75 until they were discontinued following a fatal accident. In the 1860s and '70s much social life was centred round the Literary Institute in the new Town Hall where audiences were regaled with Shakespeare by London actors, or talks on his travels by Sir John Lubbock of High Elms. Such was the demand that a School for Science and Art opened in 1878; a library was added soon afterwards. Various musical and choral societies flourished.The Drill Hall for Bromley's very active Rifle Volunteers opened in 1872 and was used besides for many varied events. Sports clubs which were established in those years have loaned a number of the illustrations reproduced in this book. There were flower shows and balls and garden parties, and the children were entertained on suitable occasions with sports days and 'treats' from church and school. And 1896 saw the inauguration of Bromley Camera Club.

Commerce was, of course, the mainspring of life in an up and coming place like Bromley. In the High Street were butcher and baker, saddler and tallow-chandler; Bromley could supply clothes, furniture, paints, even stuffed birds in glass cases. In 1882 for instance, John Howard bought an old-established grocery business opposite the *Bell*. He had but one or two assistants (says the *Bromley Record* in 1913) with a single horse and cart; yet 'today he holds the handsome and imposing range of premises known far and wide as Howard's Stores, with its 18 up-to-date departments, and an important branch at Beckenham, the firm now employing over 100 hands, with over 20 horses and vans, besides motors'. Daily deliveries were the accepted thing and Bromley's streets were full of horsecarts and handcarts, with cabs and carriages, shouts of the drivers mingling with crunching from the horses' hooves and the metal tyres of wheels on the stony surface. On market days the din was greater still. Not until evening did quiet fall.

'One of the busiest and most progressive of the independent communities within a short distance of the metropolis' is how Bromley was now described. So it is not surprising that when Local Boards were replaced by District Councils in 1894 there was talk of applying for a Charter of Incorporation as a borough. But it was not until 1902 that a crowded public meeting resolved to petition the Crown – and the resultant charter duly arrived in September 1903. The new borough celebrated with processions, ringing of bells, feasting and speechifying, with a sports day for the younger members of the community. Bromley was well practised in organising such celebrations after two royal jubilees and a coronation. The next few years saw the opening, with due ceremony and civic pride, of new municipal offices, a bigger library and the County Schools for girls and boys. In 1914 the Police Station was moved to bigger premises in Widmore Road.

That year caught the town no less and no more unprepared for war than most. Bromley Red Cross Division had been formed in 1910, although thoughts of war provoked general amusement. Nevertheless, a number of buildings were earmarked as emergency hospitals, many of them private houses. And on 14 October 1914 the first wounded arrived from Belgium – eventually some 7-8,000 'boys in blue' were to be treated in the area. As soon as war was declared a recruiting office opened opposite the post office and there were frequent recruitment meetings and rallies. Those ineligible for active service joined the Civic Guard, Special Constables (the Mayor being first to volunteer) or Bromley Civilian Training Corps. Boy Scouts guarded the railway. In September, the *District Times* published the first casualty list of six killed and 25 wounded. A year later 198 names of fatalities filled a whole page, and there was a solemn gathering on Martins Hill. Week by week the *District Times* printed personal details and often portraits of local casualties; announced citations for awards and medals; and with equal candour reported the findings of the Local Military Tribunal.

Partial blackout was ordered and advice given for air raid precautions. Later, Bromley's townsfolk watched enemy aircraft heading for the capital, and on Whit Sunday in 1918 twelve houses were damaged by a couple of bombs dropped in Queensmead and Beckenham Lane. Meanwhile there were appeals for blankets, saddles, comforts for the 'boys' and collections for munitions, guns and later, tanks. Children collected horse-chestnuts for use in the manufacture of munitions and helped with harvesting. Women took over many men's jobs. Various items of food became short, restricted, and then rationed. This was bad for most tradesmen, although Uridge's Stores was able to advertise substitutes for bread and flour. Closing of public houses morning and afternoon did not please their landlords. Bromley's communal belt was pulled tighter and tighter. By 1918 Bromley, like towns and villages all over the country, had had more than enough of the war. So peace was celebrated with one more bout of bands, bunting and speech-making. The fountain on Martins Hill was replaced by a rather splendid monument to the over 850 who had fallen in the war. Then, thankfully, Bromley turned its attention to building a land fit for heroes.

The Plates

1. Five views of Bromley, postmarked 1913 and published by Barton and Co., East Street. 'It was labour to take a photograph [in early days]; first catch your piece of glass, then cut it to registered size. Next make the sensitised emulsion and coat the glass. When ready gather up the weighty paraphernalia and trudge out.'

2. The business side of a postcard could carry a great variety of messages: 'see you at tea-time', 'father is better this morning', 'no news today on the new house'. Few people had telephones and there were several postal collections and deliveries daily. A number of Bromley stationers published postcards including Medhurst's department store. One prolific local photographer was Robert Harman.

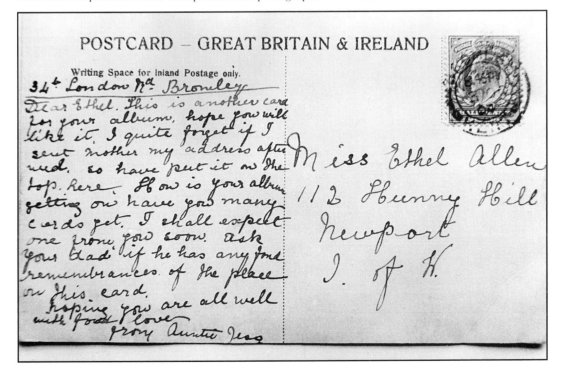

3. Bromley College, for 'twenty poore widowes of orthodox and loyall clergymen and a chaplain', was given by John Warner Bishop of Rochester in 1666, as the tablet over the entrance proclaims. Bishop Warner knew about homelessness, having been ejected from his See during the Commonwealth. Reinstated at the Restoration, he bequeathed the money for the College in his will six years later.

4. Bromley College Cloisters. An old tradition maintains that part of the College came from the ruins of the Great Fire of London. In 1978 Rev. Fergus McBride, then chaplain, argued a convincing case that the Caen stone columns which line the older quadrangle came from the first Royal Exchange in London. Another quadrangle with similar wooden columns was added c.1800.

5. The corner of Swan Hill or Beckenham Lane at about the turn of the century. The corner building was occupied by the London Cycle and Athletic Company, but advertised cars for hire! The Bromley Autocar Company had premises in West Street until a disastrous fire in 1903; it re-appeared at the top of Bromley Hill in 1921. The corner shop became a confectioner's in about 1904.

6. The top of Beckenham Lane. According to Horsburgh in 1929, the varied wares on the pavement and the group of weatherboarded cottages, overhung in springtime by clusters of wisteria blossom, all contributed to create a scene which, viewed at sunset, remained even then only as a treasured memory of picturesque old Bromley.

7. The Valley School, founded in Shortlands in 1889, began with 53 infants but numbers quickly grew. 'The opening of the Valley School', remarked the *Bromley Record* in April that year, 'has taken away one of the principal causes for the running about the parish of a number of children whose knowledge of the "three Rs" was exceedingly and unduly limited.'

8. Valley School Boys. School grants could be given towards the teaching of basic subjects, but the newly-appointed teachers for Valley School (salary £50 per annum) were told that the earning of a large grant was not to be their one great aim and they were to provide 'as good a secular instruction as circumstances would permit' and 'fit [pupils] for success in life'.

9. Shortlands Bridge before 1886 when it was replaced, following damage by floods in 1878. At that time the valley had been a sheet of water covering hedges, fences and 'even the railway which became insecure after the passing of the morning trains'. Apparently this bridge took the place of a water-splash in the later 18th century, although the perambulation of 1710 started from 'Bromley Bridge'.

10. Beating the bounds, an ancient custom which was resurrected in 1890 in the flush of civic pride making itself felt at that time. With old records to guide them, one hundred or so townsmen and boys set out from Shortlands Bridge, and returned footsore but triumphant for a celebratory meal and speechifying at the *Bell*, having blazed every tree and 'bumped' practically everybody they met on the way.

11. The *Swan and Mitre* which used to be the inn of the waggoners and carters. Now rather more up-market, it is furnished with elegant paired seats from the Gaiety Theatre in London. Although the Georgian building recently had to be restored, it maintains the atmosphere of a country town inn.

12. Upper High Street viewed from the same spot as the photograph above but facing the other way. The prominent turret, left, belongs to the *Star and Garter Inn*, rebuilt in 1898. The only major change today would be the white façade of the Odeon Cinema, just behind the gas lamp – though the lighting has changed too! This is now one of Bromley's conservation areas.

13. The *Star and Garter Inn* before it was rebuilt in exuberant Victorian black-and-white timbering. Three doors up are the premises of Thomas Wilson, the printer who published his *Accurate Description of Bromley* in 1797; later this was the home of John Dunkin, who wrote a history of the town, besides running a library and selling medicines.

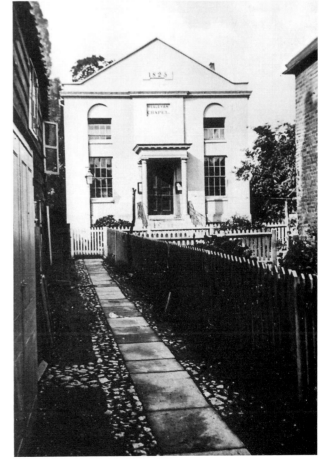

14. Zion Chapel, off the Upper High Street, up a stone-flagged passageway past cottage gardens, Horsburgh tells us, gay with flowers. The chapel, with a school-room underneath, was built in 1828. Before then Bromley's Wesleyans had met in the Market Square at a house which in 1815 had been licensed as a nonconformist meeting place to James How, watchmaker.

15.   The *Bell Hotel* in about 1890. A coaching inn recommended by Lady Catherine de Burgh in Jane Austen's *Pride and Prejudice*, it was also a local meeting place where churchwardens' pipes were laid out ready on an oval mahogany table for the regulars to 'drop in'. Foaming tankards of Allsop or Bass were supplied to customers (the publican's fellow tradesmen) through a cupboard!

16.   The *Bell Hotel*, *c*.1900. The old building became dilapidated and, after a spell propped up by wooden beams, was grandly rebuilt in 1898, as it still proudly proclaims. Quite a few of the buildings on the right-hand side survive as part of the High Street conservation area. Most of the left side was redeveloped in 1902 and the street widened.

17. This photograph shows Rawe's Academy on the right and the doctor's house on the left. By this time the once-famous school had long been closed and the premises taken over by George Sweeting, a plumber. To the house on the left had flocked the patients of 'miraculous' James Scott with their diseased joints and ulcers. Special 'Scott's Coaches' ran from London and many patients came to live in Bromley.

18. Corner of Market Square. In the centre right is the 1860s' Town Hall, presented to the town by Coles Child. Originally, the basement was used for the market and the ground floor housed offices; upstairs was the Literary Institute reading room and hall. The interior walls were pale sage green, with a cast-iron gallery and arcading in maroon. The whole cost about £10,000.

19. The parish church of St Peter and St Paul, a dedication which suggests an early foundation. Even before the bombing of 1941 there was no sign of Saxon or Norman building, except for a Norman font (which survives). Also surviving is the 15th-century tower which had been added to the medieval church. The lych gate, which looks ancient, was erected only in 1855.

20. View from Martins Hill at the end of Church Road, when the Crystal Palace dominated the skyline, but only a few houses had been built on the Shortlands ridge. In May 1858 a large crowd gathered here to watch the departure of Bromley's first train; in September 1903 another crowd cheered the reading of Bromley's Borough Charter while church bells rang.

21.   Martins Hill Recreation Ground, by long custom a place of promenade for the townsfolk. Threatened by 'the demon of bricks and mortar', the Local Board bought the land from the Church Commissioners in 1878, for £2,500. Trees were planted and flowerbeds laid out and it became the town's first ornamental park. The water fountain was donated anonymously for Queen Victoria's Diamond Jubilee.

22.   Martins Hill Gardens. This area was once a hollow, filled in by material excavated when vaults were constructed
under the north aisle of the church in 1792. After the Great War the water fountain was moved and its site used for
Bromley's war memorial; this was designed by a local family, the Longs, who also designed the war memorial of Canada.

23. The view from Queen's Mead, looking up Martins Hill across the Ravensbourne River. Both the area in the middle distance (once a hop garden) and the meadow across the stream were acquired for the town for £4,600 to celebrate the Queen's Golden Jubilee in 1887. This lower, more level, stretch of land was used for sports and games. From 1911, Queen's Mead Bowling Club used this site.

24. Jubilee bonfire, 22 July 1897. Thousands assembled on Martins Hill to witness the bonfire which formed the climax to the day's festivities. There was no wind so the flames shot up to a great height, brightly illuminating the 'animated and striking scene'. Celebrations had begun with a procession of decorated vehicles and cycles (in which Satterthwaite's Springhill Dairy won a prize) and an afternoon of sports.

25. The Ravensbourne with a diminutive but hopeful fisherman and his admirer. Once trout abounded in clear water, but pollution spread upstream from the factories of Deptford and Lewisham, and the last noble fish to be caught is accredited to Joseph Wells, father of 'H.G.'. Until about 1830 the Ravensbourne powered Bromley mill, last used in the manufacture of glass.

26. 'A brake full of helpers' set out on 14 August 1906 for the annual workhouse outing organised by Charles Gedney to High Elms, Downe. There everyone enjoyed a picnic and the children were given sweets and toys. Afterwards there were games – punctuated by slight showers – before returning after a generous tea. But this picture might be Valley Tennis Club off on *their* annual outing!

27. Church House was the name given to Bromley's rectory from the Reformation onwards, when it was leased to tenants. Until the mid-19th century a substantial group of farm buildings stood next to Church Road. The house was rebuilt c.1830 (with additions such as the turret some 50 years later) and extensive pleasure grounds laid out with lawns sloping to the lake.

28. The Church from the south-west. The south aisle was part of the medieval Gothic church, although the windows have been altered more than once. Chancel and chancel aisle were added, after a good deal of controversy, by public subscription in 1884, and vestries with an organ chamber above on the north. The architect of these additions was Sir Thomas Jackson, R.A.

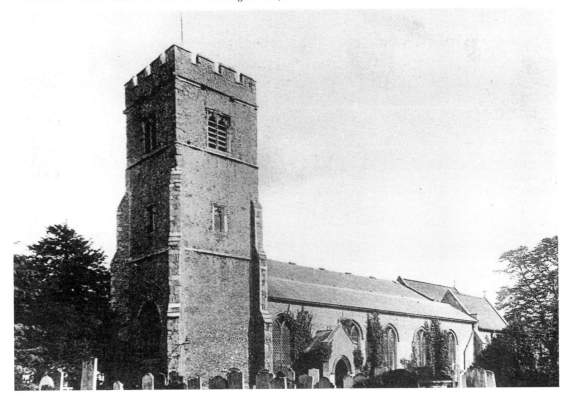

29. Bromley church interior after 1892 when the alabaster reredos was added. This was designed by the architect and depicted the Last Supper. The east window was richly traced, reminiscent of Kentish tracery. The centre light represented the Crucifixion; to one side was the Adoration of the Magi and the Shepherds and to the other, the Resurrection; St Peter and St Paul stood at either end. The 18th-century pews were removed and the church reseated in 1873.

30. A quiet glimpse through the north door. The door in the south porch was described in Hone's *Table Book* (1839) as 'a good specimen of the fast-decaying fine doors of our old churches'. Sadly, it was lost in the bombing but another survives in the tower, its blank tracery and style of woodwork indicating a 14th-century date.

31. Opposite the *Bell* the High Street widens into a triangle, perhaps the original market place. In the centre was a drinking fountain surmounted by a lamp which is now (minus lamp) on Hayes Common. Behind stood Church Row in Georgian brick, venue of solicitors and doctors before commerce took over. On the corner is Covell's new shop, which later became Midland Bank.

32. Covell's old shop. The Covell family was the last in a long line of butchers on this site, stretching back to at least the 17th century when John Giles' property was rated at £4. James Covell bought it in 1861 and the business prospered sufficiently for him to be able to replace this building in substantial Victorian brick some 20 years afterwards.

33. Traffic jam – in the days when the butchers still did their own slaughtering, and the sheep and cattle were driven to the abattoir up the High Street. There are accounts told of how shepherds and their dogs had a job to keep their charges from diving off down the side turnings – as if they realised the fate awaiting them.

34. New Cut. The west side of the Square became very encroached upon early in the last century. Narrow and squalid, it was dubbed the Back Alley. Coaches and other through traffic had to turn left then right past the old Market House. After much discussion a widening scheme produced what was then called 'New Cut', and solved the traffic problem.

35. Market Square, north side. Behind the imposing portico, left, was originally an 18th-century inn called, initially, the *Queen's Head* and later the *Bull*; upstairs there was a large and elegant assembly room. In the 1790s it became a butcher's shop, bought by W.F. Skilton in 1905. Opposite stands Bromley's parish pump in its original position.

36. The Old Market House which was demolished in the 1860s. By this time the townspeople were referring to it as 'our old shed' and it was clearly out of keeping with Bromley's new, prosperous image. There is no record of it being built but it was probably in about 1739 when Peter Burrell of Beckenham leased the market tolls.

37. Uridge's Corner before this entrance to the Square was widened in 1883. Uridge's moved to new premises in Widmore Road where the name is still visible on the side wall of their 'handsome, commodious and splendidly appointed shop ... which employs a large staff whose unremitting efforts are constantly devoted to catering for the requirements of the public' (*Industrial Great Britain 1890*).

38. The end of Widmore Road with the
entrance to Market Square on the left, before
1880 when the *Prince of Wales* on the corner
became the estate office of Waterer and,
later, Dickens. In 1913 this and the old
cottages were demolished to ease access that
side and make way for the Post Office. The
streets were gaslit by now and the surface
gravelled.

39. Bromley Post Office. The present
building was erected in 1897 and enlarged in
1913, by which time the indoor staff had
increased from three to 24 and delivery men
more than five-fold. Previously the Post
Office was in Middle Row in the Square, and
before that in a long series of shops and inns.

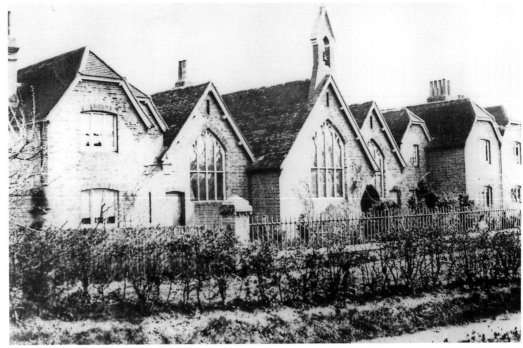

40.   Bromley Parish Schools cost £2,700 when built in 1855 to replace the old buildings at Masons Hill, nearly half raised by public subscription. There were separate schoolrooms for boys, girls and infants, with houses for both master and mistress. After coming under Bromley School Board for some years they became elementary schools under the new Education Committee in 1902.

41.   Bromley Football Club was formed in 1892. They first played at Plaistow between Glebe Road and College Road – the site of the public entrance is still traceable opposite the present market. This early group photograph seems to have been taken on their more northerly pitch, where Ronalds and Holligrave Roads are now, between 1900 and 1905.

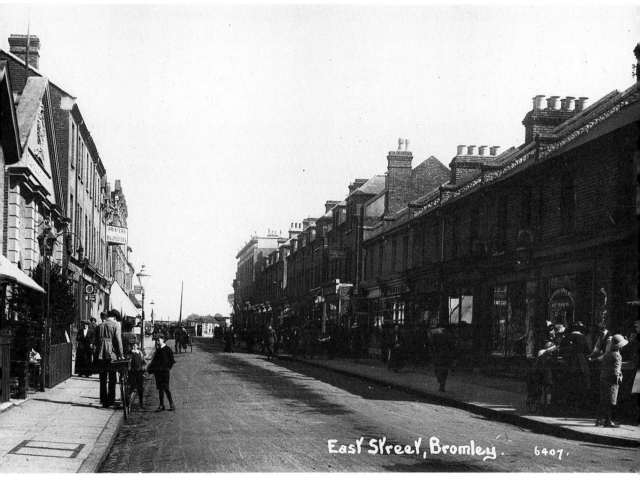

East Street, Bromley. 6407.

42.   East Street. North, South, East and West Streets were laid out in the 1870s. From 1878 East Street led to Bromley's railway station. On the left, with the badge of the Royal West Kent Regiment on the gable, is the Drill Hall which was opened in 1872 for Bromley Volunteer Rifle Corps, and used by many other organisations besides.

43. Bromley Camera Club met at the Drill Hall in their early days, later at the *White Hart* and the Carnegie Library where they were allowed to use the cellars as dark rooms. Here, they are on an outing to West Wickham (probably in 1897), the photograph being taken by Mr. S.B. Webber. Meetings are now held at the United Reformed church.

44. Samuel B. Webber, first President of Bromley Camera Club, which he founded in 1896. Mr. Webber was a specialist in church interiors and one of his photographs of St Mary's church, Plaistow (the east window presented by Lady Scott in memory of her husband), is reproduced in E.L.S. Horsburgh's *Bromley*. This picture of him, taken in 1890 by an unknown photographer, is entitled 'Feeding Fowls'.

45. The chancel of St George's church, Bickley, photographed by Samuel Webber. A similar picture of the altar at Bromley parish church has the note: 'Exposure *130 minutes*, Aperture F22. Yellow Screen No.2. ISO plate'.

46. The Misses Cawston, daughters of Samuel Cawston, at Bromley Hill (now *Bromley Court Hotel*). The gardens, which had been landscaped earlier in the century by Lady Farnborough, were a great attraction in Victorian times. This photograph may well have featured in the first Camera Club Exhibition which was held at Collings' Art Gallery in the Upper High Street on 20 January 1906.

47. Bromley Volunteer Rifle Corps photographed in the early 1900s. The Corps, formed at the time of the Crimean War, became a battalion of the Territorial Army and saw active service in 1914-18. After 1872 they had their Drill Hall in East Street and a rifle range near Grove Park where they held frequent competitions. Everybody who was anybody (among the men folk) in the town belonged.

48. Bromley and West Kent Fanciers used the Drill Hall for their annual show. Here is Henry J. Wilson who won the 'best team' cup from 1886-91. In 1917 he had his picture taken with his array of prizes and photographs of the winning birds – a redwing on the left and a mistle thrush on the right. He claimed his oldest bird, a starling, was 70.

49. Widmore Road. The impressive building in the centre is the Congregational chapel of 1881. Beyond was a row of Georgian town houses. To the right of the chapel is the *Three Compasses*, rebuilt in 1911. Next come two shops, much admired when new in 1872. On the far right is Curwood's Stationery Stores – this illustration is from one of their own postcards.

50. The Congregational chapel in Widmore Road, erected in 1835 when Bethel chapel in Centenary Place became too small (before that the Congregationalists met in a house in Isard's Yard off the Market Square). By 1880 the Widmore chapel was itself inadequate for all its multifarious activities and was replaced by the large handsome building seen opposite.

51. The No. 109 bus in Widmore Road. On 1 June 1914 the London General Omnibus Company opened its garage at Catford and commenced a 15-minute service from Bromley to Penge. In August, on the outbreak of war, the garage was requisitioned by the army and this service suspended – to be resumed in August 1916 and extended to Woolwich to serve the Arsenal (until 1919).

52. On 25 September 1907 the new Municipal Buildings, a handsome and imposing block of offices, were opened by the Mayor in the presence of an influential body of burgesses. The Mayor is seen here stepping forward to receive a key from the architect, Mr. R.F. Atkinson.

53. A huge gathering collected to hear Mayor Alderman Thomas Davis, J.P., proclaim on 9 May 1910 that Prince George Frederick Ernest Albert 'has now, by the death of our late Sovereign of Happy Memory, become our only lawful and rightful Liege Lord'. The crowd gave a rousing cheer and the National Anthem was sung with great gusto. Before Bromley became a Borough, such proclamations were not customary in the town.

54. The Baptist church and Free Library; the Library was added to the School for Science and Art in 1894. The Baptist chapel opened in 1865. Although Baptist meetings had been held for some time it was not until Archibald Brown became minister that a permanent church was felt necessary. Between the two buildings runs an ancient field path, now enclosed.

55. The first Phillips Memorial Hospital was opened in 1889 at the junction of Park Road with Widmore Road in memory of a well-loved homeopathic doctor. The demand for treatment exceeded the resources on that site and in 1900 the second Phillips Memorial Hospital was opened adjacent to Queen's Gardens. Even that had to be enlarged a few years later.

56. The Homeopathic Hospital and Queen's Gardens. both sited on what had been White Hart Field which, from time immemorial, had been a part of the outdoor life of the town. Bromley Cricket Club, in particular, played here for many years. Coles Child presented its freehold to the townspeople to commemorate Queen Victoria's Diamond Jubilee, on condition that it became a public garden.

57. Boy Scout blowing the 'All clear' on the roof of the police station, c.1915. 'They were splendid', declares the Congregational Church War History, 'careering about in the small hours of the morning with their cheerful bugle calls, assuring us the raiders had been driven home.' Warning of air raids was given by firing maroons next to the fire station.

58. Bromley Naturalists' Society, founded in 1888 by William Baxter and Rev. H. Soames. Besides outings such as this (perhaps to Greenwich) in 1895, the Society held regular meetings at the Literary Institute and occasional exhibitions. They also formed a collection of books and specimens which, unfortunately, had to be dispersed when the Society was disbanded on the outbreak of war in 1914.

59. Fire in the Market Square draws the crowds. In June 1909 it took nine fire engines (from Perry Green to Farnborough stations) and 43 firemen two hours to put this one out. One elderly resident of Cooper's Cottages died of shock. This view is from the rear in Widmore Road, along the alley between the Congregational church and *Three Compasses*.

60. Postcard of the 1909 fire, which obviously caused great excitement. Just as obviously the photograph has been 'improved' to show flames that, by then, must have died down! In the centre is Dunn's furnishing shop, established in Bromley from the early 18th century; later they built a new store on the site of the cottages to the right.

61. Bromley Palace, for centuries a residence of the Bishops of Rochester. The present house was built in 1775, although the pillared walkway at the rear and the dormer windows were added by Coles Child when he bought the estate. The grounds were even then only a fraction of what they had been and only part of the encircling moat survived.

62. Palace Farm. Every large estate depended on its own farm produce, and this was true of Bromley Palace. The farm buildings, including the large brick storage barn, were across the paddock from the mansion. Hops were once grown locally although the soil is nowhere really rich. Oasts, barns and other buildings were demolished in 1927 to make way for a housing estate.

63. The Market has been held on Thursdays since 1447 and on Tuesdays before that, since the time of King John's charter of 1205. This would have been nullified if only one market day was missed, so whenever Christmas Day fell on a Thursday one solitary stall was set up for a short while. Some time in the mid-19th century the market actually ceased, but was later revived.

64. Edward Strong, seen here with his family, established his printing firm in 1857 in the *White Hart*. The following year he published Bromley's first newspaper to coincide with the opening of the railway, for which he included timetables, and also a short history of the town. Afterwards he moved to the Market Square. From 1866, continuing after Edward's death in 1875 until 1906, the firm issued a yearly directory.

LOCAL FOOD CONTROL OFFICE

65. Market Day: the Thursday pedestrianisation of Market Square, long before one-way traffic was thought of. And what better place for the wartime Local Food Control Office in the adjacent Town Hall? In the distance is the building erected as offices by the Local Board in 1867, which by this time had become the estate agency of Baxter, Payne and Lepper. This card is postmarked 1925, but the photograph was obviously taken during the war.

66. Sanger's Circus in procession through the Market Square in September 1898: 'dear to the hearts of the younger generation' declares the *Bromley Chronicle*, and to many of their elders for that matter! This 'Greatest and Grandest Exhibition' included lady clowns, camels, and elephants. The latter entertained the public by playing football against the clowns. Entrance cost between 6d. and 3s.

67. The west side of Market Place. Half-way along the shops, on the left, was the china shop of Joseph Wells, H.G.'s birthplace. Joseph also sold cricket gear and was in fact a professional with West Kent Cricket Club for some years. A fast round-hand bowler, he played for Kent for two seasons. His shop became part of Fred Medhurst's, Bromley's first departmental store.

68. Market Square from the south. When 'New Cut' was made the bay-fronted building was added to the central block. Used as a police station for some 20 years until that was moved to the new Town Hall in 1864, it then became the *Forester Inn*, though just round the corner were the *Rose and Crown* and the *Duke's Head*.

69. Our Tank, 'Drake', came to Bromley in March 1918 for three days and caused a sensation. The streets were decorated with bunting, bands played, speeches were made, and the citizens of Bromley queued to buy War Bonds with a special Tank Stamp on them. The target was to raise £100,000, enough for a submarine, but in the event £176,000 was collected.

70. Payne's Corner, taken over from the *Forester*. Although the centre of the Square was rebuilt in 1932, Payne's still have premises here, complete with a smaller clock hanging proudly outside. The motor bus is one of the early No. 47s, Thomas Tilling's route from Shoreditch to Lewisham, which was motorised in 1912 and extended to Bromley.

71. The *White Hart*, right, existed in Bromley from at least the 16th century. Later one of the two coaching inns, it is reputed to have had stabling for 100 horses. In about 1830 it was rebuilt further back with a forecourt and a spacious assembly room was added. Until the Town Hall was erected it was the usual venue for all sorts of public functions.

72. 'All for me': a strange way to celebrate the wedding of Edward Prince of Wales to Princess Alexandra, although somewhat less eccentric then than now, was the gastronomic feat of Peter Nesbitt. As a public spectacle outside the *White Hart* he consumed a giant pie, specially made from 4lb. pastry and 5lb. beef, and washed it down with a gallon of beer.

73. An earlier view of the *White Hart*, showing the south wing (right) which was leased separately as a tap, or off-licence, and the elegant north wing, then the chemist's shop of Edward Gould and the recognised homeopathic centre for the district. In about 1902 this entrance to the Square was widened and the north wing replaced by the shops in plate 71. Note the elegant lamps.

74.   The volunteer fire brigade was established in 1868 at a public meeting in the Town Hall and was initially manned
by members of the Rifle Volunteers. Their new up-to-date engine was housed at the *White Hart* where horses could be
quickly provided. A steam engine, garaged in West Street, succeeded it in 1897. In 1904 the voluntary system was
disbanded and a new fire station built.

75. Two Bromley tradesmen almost opposite the *White Hart* were Bush and Baxter. Originally a bookseller, Samuel Bush added printing to his business, publishing a *Bromley Directory* from 1894 to 1914. There were three generations of William Baxters. The first opened this chemist's shop in 1820; his grandson sold it in 1907, perhaps to make more time for his great hobby – the history of Bromley.

76. High Street further south. Although many shops still carry exterior lights, Bromley now has gas street lighting. The tall chimney is at Bromley's own electricity works, opened in 1898. The first to experiment by lighting a shop window with electricity was the youngest William Baxter, who rigged up a series of batteries; but after one hour of splendour, there was a 'grand smash-up'!

77. Aberdeen Buildings were erected in 1894-8 south of several private houses, later also converted into shops. It was an imposing range with spacious accommodation above the shops, appropriate to the town's growing success and importance. In November 1914, during the Great War, part of the building was opened as a recreation centre and canteen for the many soldiers billeted in the town.

78. The public library, opposite Aberdeen Buildings, was opened in 1906 by the philanthropist Andrew Carnegie, who donated £7,500 for the building. The site had been bequeathed to the town by Mrs. Emily Dowling for a public museum or 'some kind of institution or establishment for public benefit'. The extensive grounds of the house, 'Neelgherries', were laid out as the 'Library Gardens'.

79. The Wesleyan chapel, built to replace Zion Chapel off the Upper High Street when it became too small for the congregation. The opening of the new chapel in November 1876 was celebrated in sober manner by a series of seven special sermons by visiting preachers, some of them former pastors in Bromley.

Wesleyan Chapel & High Street, Bromley.

80. Lower High Street. The Broadway, begun in 1885 and completed some 20 years later, drew many businesses from the old town centre. Before about 1870 there was a high bank on both sides of the road. Behind the eastern bank stood Bromley Lodge and to the west was Bromley House. Then three new roads of middle-class villas were laid out on the Bromley House estate.

81.   Bromley Conservative Club, shown here on an outing to Oxted in about 1898. The club met originally above an estate agency in Market Square, but in 1884 moved to the Broadway where there was room for billiards and a bar. The Conservatives had a subsidiary Debating Society and an Athletics Club which held its first annual dinner in 1897. This was preceded by a 4½-mile race, presumably to raise a good appetite!

82. The Broadway. Bromley Lodge estate was not developed until the 1880s when more roads, with larger villas, were built in the grounds and the 'garden front' sold off to make way for the parade of shops. The 18th-century Lodge itself remained, with access through an archway between two shops, and became the home of Bromley Conservative Club.

83. Charter Mayor's coach: crowds lined the High Street in glorious sunshine as the Charter deputation returned to Bromley on 21 September 1903 in a special carriage attached to the Holborn train. The procession formed as escort to Queen's Mead included trumpeters of the Royal Horse Artillery, Bromley Volunteer Band and Companies, the fire brigade with their engine, and many town dignitaries in their carriages.

84.   Bromley South station. Bromley's own first station was opened in 1858, two months after the one at Shortlands where the first trains terminated. The original station building and a stationmaster's house were set beside the line on the south side. The station building was re-sited on the bridge in 1894 and the access way was absorbed into the goods yard.

85.   Steaming through Bromley: Europa Class 2-4-0 *Asia*. In the 1880s there were about 15 trains from Charing Cross each weekday with another 12 from Cannon Street, and over 40 to Victoria. A first-class return ticket cost 2s. 3d., the third-class being one shilling less; the introduction of the cheaper early morning workman's fare was resisted for many years on the line.

86. Bromley South station from the south. The stationmaster was provided with a house, as was the practice, next to the station; in her later years Florence Nightingale often visited friends at Keston and would write to him to reserve one compartment for her maid and the luggage, and another for herself 'because of my ill-health'.

87. Simpson's Road, beyond the railway, in contrast to the other new roads up the hill, was developed as artisan housing – largely terraced, with narrow frontages. A few small shops were included. The road was named after nearby Simpson's Place which, by the late 19th century, had become a romantic and rather mysterious ruin. The tower belongs to St Mark's.

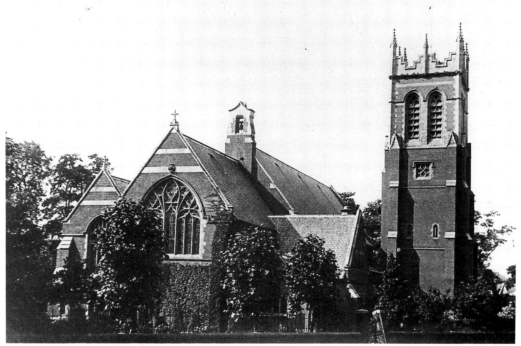

88. St Mark's church, consecrated in 1898 as a chapel-of-ease to the parish church, was needed to accommodate the rapidly expanding population in south Bromley. Money for the site was given by Eley Soames of Ravenscroft and Thomas Dewey of South Hill House (later Bromley's Charter Mayor); at a fund-raising Grand Bazaar held in Bromley Palace grounds, stalls 'displayed considerable taste and ingenuity'.

89. The interior of St Mark's church was furnished according to the architect's ideas. Organ and pulpit came from the Iron Church. Stalls for clergy and choir, along with the lectern, were given by the Dewey family. Other members of the congregation gave seats for the sedilia, altar rail and font. In 1901 Miss Wishart provided the stained-glass east window.

90. The first St Mark's church, with furniture and fittings, was given by Samuel Cawston, who lived at Bromley Hill House. Known as the Iron Church or 'tin tabernacle', it was erected in 1884 for the use of those who, until then, had been attending worship in the Masons Hill Schools across the road. During the Great War it was used as a soldiers' club.

91. Masons Hill Schools opened in November 1872. Initially, the older children were taken to Sunday services at St John's church in New Bromley. A stream ran beside the school, and after heavy rain in 1878 the flood destroyed part of the wall. In 1911 the building was demolished to allow for road widening and the school was re-sited south of the stream.

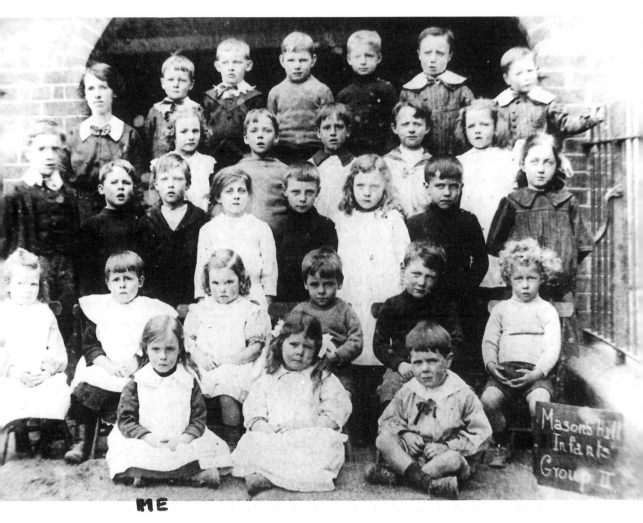

92.   Masons Hill School infants, *c.*1914. ME was Kitty Ling, aged about five. She was born in 1909 and started school in 1912! Her brother, two years older, stands behind. Back row: Munkton brothers, Blanchard, Webb, Lee, Lee. Fourth row: Miss Betts, Smith, Haffenden, Hackney, Krantz, Fox, Third row: -?-, Goad, Jeffries, -?-, Ling, Morris, Webb, Mason. Second row: Jeffries, Hackney, -?-, Haffenden, Mason, Webb. Front row: Ling, Goad, Trindall.

93. Widening Masons Hill further up was approved in January 1906 at a cost of £922, less than an earlier estimate because Eley Soames had offered to donate a strip of his frontage in exchange for a retaining wall and new gates. Added employment in the Borough was welcomed, especially as that winter the workhouse Guardians were unable to give the unemployed stone-breaking work.

94. Bromley High School made a great impact on girls' education in the town. Established by the Girls' Public Day School Trust to be a place 'not only of instruction but of education in the true sense of the word', it opened in 1883 with 24 pupils and grew rapidly under Miss Heppel, who brought to the school a high standard of scholarship and a strong linguistic bias.

95. Gym class at Bromley High School shortly before 1914, during the time Miss Mabel Agnew Hodge was headmistress. An old girl recalls: 'We had Swedish Drill taught by Miss Campbell, a fierce, robust lady with very short hair. I'm sure she was really very kind, but she seemed to copy the famous army drill sergeants'.

96. Bromley Cottage Hospital. In 1869 the editor of the *Bromley Record* drew the attention of readers to an advertisement 'from which they will see that an effort is being made to establish a cottage hospital for the benefit of Bromley and the surrounding districts'. Those efforts were successful, for two small cottages were soon purchased and a six-bed hospital prepared for patients.

97. The rear of Bromley Cottage Hospital. The cottages were demolished in 1875 and this building erected; but demand continued to increase and the hospital was expanded three times before 1910, by which time there were 42 beds and over 3,500 patients had been treated. In the early days patients were only accepted on the recommendation of the hospital's donors and subscribers.

98. 'J. Morton Crouch, ironmonger', whose name, together with those of three public houses in the Masons Hill area inspired the following riddle: Q. Why did Morton Crouch? A. Because the Two Brewers gave the Railway signal there was a Tiger on the Hill! (*The Tiger's Head*, the only survivor, alas).

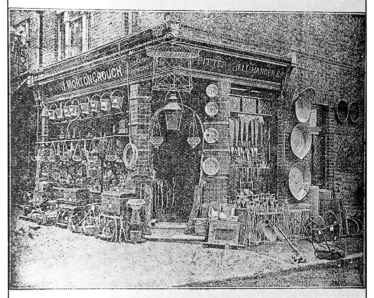

J. MORTON CROUCH,

Furnishing and Builders' Ironmonger.

Latest and most Improved Machinery for Grinding Lawn Mowers. Any make repaired equal to new.

EFFICIENT STAFF OF WORKMEN FOR ALL REPAIRS.

PLUMBING, GASFITTING, ELECTRIC LIGHT AND BELLS, PAINTING, CARPENTERING, &c.

PERSONAL SUPERVISION.

41, Masons Hill & 25, Widmore Road, Bromley.

(NEAR L. C. & D. RY. STATION.)

Telephone 98 Bromley.

99. Top of Masons Hill. Masons Hill was one of Bromley parish's five separate ancient hamlets, and half a mile from the old town. Originally agricultural, it became more industrial with carpenters' shops and blacksmiths' forges. The nearer building on the right may have been part of a Tudor farmhouse, with even older timbers incorporated into it.

100. The beginning of 'Bromley Common'. A Miss Milstead, reminiscing to the *Bromley Times* in 1923, recalled the road south from the town across what had once been Bromley Common as quiet and peaceful, except for the occasional cart or the horn of a coach; in May there was a profusion of chestnut, lilac, laburnum and other trees bright with blossom, and cuckoos could be heard.

101. Wendover Road, off Masons Hill, was laid out in about 1900 on a 'greenfield site', and became a street of gracious Edwardian houses, very different from the Victorian terraces and three-storey villas elsewhere. The road leads to a bridge over the railway which replaced the older Ivy Bridge after it collapsed in 1882, killing seven workmen and injuring another in a hut underneath.

102. Bromley County School for Boys opened in September 1911 with 72 boys and room for 300, having 10 classrooms, a laboratory, art room and gymnasium, with a rented field for games. Five masters answered the call to colours three years later including housemaster (Captain) Grails who lost his life at Gallipoli; two others were also killed, as were five 'old boys'.

103. The *Five Bells* on Bromley Common which, before enclosure in 1821, was 300 acres of rough, wet wasteland and a notorious haunt of highwaymen. The main highway skirted all this past Hook Farm to the *Crown*, where it soon divided, the Westerham road running past the Rookery and then Oakley to Keston Mark, the Tonbridge road continuing southwards via the *Plough Inn*.

104. Raglan Road junior classroom in 1914. The school was opened in 1889. Three teachers from the Senior Boys' department joined up in 1914, and were replaced by the first women teachers to be appointed. One of the three was awarded the Military Cross in September 1917; in October another resumed his post having been invalided out of the army.

105. Ambulance training began well before the war. In July 1913 Hayes Common was scattered with battle casualties, some terribly injured, judging by their labels. St John's Ambulance Brigade rendered first aid before transporting them, via a clearing station at Hayes School staffed by Red Cross nurses, to Masons Hill School – transformed into a 25-bed hospital complete with isolation ward freely disinfected with Lysol.

106. St Luke's church was built for the growing population of Bromley Common in 1886, of red brick, though the spire added later was of stone from Somerset. The Shooting Common Post Office near the church derives its name from one-time local archery butts – or perhaps from the dangers of the Common!

107. The *Crown Inn* moved across the road in about 1866 when the older site was absorbed into the grounds of Elmfield House. Once known as 'The Pye House', it was the 'last services' before the open common, complete with pond, watertrough and haytrough, and a reputation for good ale. The Norman family expanded their Elmfield estate throughout the 18th and 19th centuries.

108. The Rookery, the first house on the site, dated *c.*1660, was pulled down and replaced in the early 18th century. Purchased by James Norman in 1764, the house was improved and extended by various members of the family but was destroyed by fire in 1946. The estate came to include most of Bromley Common.

109. Holy Trinity, the first church to be built on Bromley Common, was completed in 1841 and a tower added in 1843. The exterior flintwork is of a remarkable quality. The yew trees by the road were planted by the first vicar. To the rear the old buildings were originally the church school and master's house. The Norman family have been great benefactors to the parish.

110. Oakley House was possibly an old inn on the road to Westerham, situated on a slight rise. The house was bought by George Norman in 1825, then altered and extended by local builders W. Smith and Sons, who also added wards for the V.A.D. hospital in 1916. During World War Two it was commandeered by the armed forces and a large gymnasium added.

111. The Bromley Corps of Kent Voluntary Aid Detachment was formed from the Red Cross, St John's Ambulance and the Territorial Force Association to render first aid and liaise between Field and Base Hospitals. Women in particular wanted to support the fighting men by being usefully occupied in rolling bandages and making soft slippers for hospital use, as shown in this photograph.

112. Oakley Road, where little has changed in the last 90 years except for the loss of trees. Some of the shops have now been converted to private accommodation. The *Two Doves* still remains; formerly there was a small beer house almost next door called the *Vine*.

113. Gravel Road derives its name from the extraction of gravel, used in improving the main Hastings Road, from the site of the present recreation ground. At No. 4 lived William Smith the builder. It was his son George, a member of the Quarter-Plate Negative Club of Great Britain, who took these photographs – this one in 1887 from outside the *Bird in Hand*.

114. Skim Corner, on the edge of the common, was passed by the old road to Tonbridge en route to Crofton and Farnborough. The house on the left is of typical Kentish design and the brick cottages were formerly a small beer house. Both still remain. Skim Corner is now part of Jackson Road.

115. The main Hastings Road about 70 years ago, with only an early motorbus and a horse van to be seen. Bromley Common Post Office and shops remain largely unaltered. Jackson Road derives its name from the shop on the corner. A short distance further towards Bromley the *Sawyer's Arms* took its name from a saw pit where timber was cut by hand.

116. The *Plough Inn* (left) replaced an earlier inn on the same site, with its pond just beyond under the willows; and round the corner in Cherry Orchard Road was a blacksmith's forge. The *Plough* became headquarters of the Princes Plain Cricket Club when it was formed in 1812, and a stretch of marshy common was drained and cleared for their pitch.

117. 'To the relief of Hastings!' on 17 March 1909 when Mafeking was fresh in mind: an exercise in motorised transport by the Brigade of Guards. A curious and excited crowd gathered to watch the novel and stirring sight (reported the *Bromley Record*), the low, powerful yet quiet vehicles only a few yards apart, each carrying from two to six guardsmen muffled in their greatcoats.

118. Turpington Farm, a timber-framed house which dates from the late 14th century, a rare pre-Wealden hall-house with its separately roofed and jettied wings. Horse races were run here in the 18th century, which local tradition claims were attended by Frederick, Prince of Wales. In 1734 the prize offered for the 'big race' was 25 guineas.

119. Haymakers – a reminder of Bromley's agricultural hinterland. Farm holdings varied in size from a few acres to hundreds. With 19th-century improvements in transport, local produce was increasingly diversified away from cereals, pulse, meat and orchard fruits (with a few hops) by the introduction of soft fruits, potatoes, vegetables and dairying. However agricultural fortunes fluctuated, one important item was hay for the horses.

120. Southborough was one of Bromley's hamlets, just east of Bromley Common. There was a water-splash across Southborough Lane here, with a little wooden bridge for pedestrians. This stream flowed north to serve the gasworks, then west – past Masons Hill School – to the Ravensbourne. A blacksmith's forge and the weatherboarded *Chequers Inn* stood together, with a large thatched barn which housed horses and a carriage.

121. The *Crooked Billet*, at Southborough opposite the end of Blackbrook Lane, was, in about 1882, a picturesque building which had once been a farm. It had a parlour window street shop, a joy to the children. There were fields of waving grass and the delights of haytime, orchards, and nearby fields of raspberries and strawberries destined for the London markets.

122. Widmore, another of the ancient hamlets, stood at the important junction of Widmore Lane with Plaistow Lane. A cluster of houses great and small with an inn and at one time a pond where, reputedly, there was once a ducking stool, it was known, until late last century, as Wigmore. The row of cottages half way up the hill are Beechfield Cottages.

123. Widmore Road, looking back towards Bromley. Beechfield Cottages have been partly masked by a row of shops. Just visible among the trees are the chimneys of Beechfield House. When a Dr. Roberts built his new house here on the site of an ancient farm he justified its name by planting one green- and one copper-beech tree in the grounds.

124. The Old Gateway in Bickley Road proclaims its building date as 1599. Set behind is 'The Old Cottage' which is probably contemporary – a timber-framed house with red brick infill and a porch. It is Grade II nationally listed for preservation. Almost opposite, where its inn sign can be seen, is the 18th-century *Bird-in-Hand* public house.

125. St George's church was built in 1864-5 to serve the growing population of the prestigious Bickley Park estate development, and was largely financed by the developer as an added amenity. Horsburgh praises it as a notable addition to the churches of Kent but Pevsner, the architectural historian, dislikes the interior arcades, describing them as 'cruelly hideous and inappropriate'! The tower was rebuilt in about 1905.

126. The Water Tower on Summer Hill is actually in Chislehurst but is part of Bromley history, having been built to serve Bickley Park. It also acted as a lodge when the road beyond was a private drive, the highway being Old Hill. In 1870 the developer was able to advertise his new road to Bickley station, 'first class houses', a cricket ground and gas laid on.

127. Sundridge Park: a part of the manor of Bromley which seems to have become separated in medieval times. By 1792 it was known as Washer's-in-the-Woods; that year Claude Scott bought the estate and he employed Humphry Repton to make improvements. A copy of his *Red Book*, containing sketches of the park and his proposed alterations, is now in Bromley Library.

128. Sundridge Mansion. Originally employed to improve the grounds, Repton insisted that the house should also be rebuilt, on a south-facing slope with 'a rich background of woods ... and a beautiful valley to east and west'. Highly classical, John Nash had some say in the early plans but Repton completed the work. The Scott family were prominent benefactors throughout the 19th century.

129.   Plaistow Lane: the Widmore Green end. Behind the trees is No. 107, one of the houses designed in 1902 by Ernest Newton, a pupil of Richard Norman Shaw. Bromley's outer fringes – especially Bickley – are significant as the cradle of the Arts-and-Crafts architectural style developed by Shaw and his followers in the later 19th century, a return to brick and half-timbered gables.

130.   Bromley Cricket Club began in the early 19th century but became extinct during the 'hungry forties'. It was re-kindled in 1856 by Joseph Wells and police sergeant Stubberfield (seated with bat) and has flourished ever since. The earliest known photograph, taken on 28 July 1866, shows the Club against N.C.O.s of the Royal Artillery. The team played on the White Hart Field, today's Queen's Gardens.

131. Cycle track racing gradually took over from road racing. In August 1890 a popular series of races began at Bromley Cricket Ground (as here, lined up for the start) but Club members competed – and won – at Herne Hill, Catford and Crystal Palace. In 1902 the Club became the Bromley Cycle and Motor-cycle Club but was disbanded in 1912.

132. The Cricket Club pavilion, built in 1902 and costing £690, at the ground in Plaistow Lane to which the Club moved in 1886. Behind the committee's announcement 'the new pavilion is now completed though not without a good deal of trouble to themselves' can be detected a welter of work ... collecting donations, a tax on subscriptions, even a production of *The Mikado* 'on a Napoleonic scale'.

133. Bromley Hockey Club. Following its move to Plaistow Lane, Bromley Cricket Club tried Rugby Football as a winter pastime but after three seasons found this unsatisfactory. On 28 September 1889 Bromley Hockey Club was founded and has continued on the same pitch ever since. This 1891-2 photograph showing founder member H.J. Green (seated, right) is the earliest on record.

134. Hockey match v. Teddington at Plaistow in 1909: a rare action photograph. This was during a less successful epoch than when they were Champions of the South – in 1897, 1898 and again in 1900. The new decade brought a number of new members and Bromley was scoring victories again when war was declared in 1914 and the game formally discontinued for the duration.

135. St Joseph's Roman Catholic church: the original corrugated iron chapel which superseded a temporary chapel in London Road and, like it, was served from St Mary's at Chislehurst. In 1911 this building was replaced in Romanesque yellow brick, with a gallery at the west end for the use of Holy Trinity Convent, the parent body.

136. Freelands was one of the smaller estates surrounding the old market town and records of its ownership go back to the reign of Henry VIII. From 1818-88 it was part of the Sundridge Estate. The right half of the present mansion was built early in the 18th century and another block, in matching style, was added early in the present century.

137.   Holy Trinity Convent: sisters and pupils outside Freelands in the early days of the school. The Trinitarian sisters had moved to Bromley in 1886, first to a house in London Road called Willow Bank; they purchased Freelands two years later for £13,000. The school quickly became popular, gaining a reputation for sound teaching, and the building had to expand to cope with growing numbers.

138.   Lady Scott's Infants' School. On 1 March 1880 the *Bromley Record* reported: 'Mr. Edward H. Scott has just erected in Sundridge Park an Infant School ... of red brick, prettily ornamented ... to accommodate 85-6 children. It was opened on February 19th when 50 parents were invited ... Mr. and Mrs. Scott did all in their power to render their visitors happy and comfortable.'

139.   Bromley Bowling Club had been inaugurated in the Spring of 1888 by a band of enthusiasts meeting in a private room at the busy *Bell Hotel*, and soon acquired a site for a bowling green behind Lady Scott's Infant's School. Initially membership was limited to 50, most of whom were leading local businessmen, and the Club was, for a time, rather more social than serious. This photograph was taken in 1894.

140.   Bowls match, 1901. That year a party of New Zealand and Australian bowlers visited England; Bromley's committee made them honorary members and two friendly matches were played at Plaistow Lane. Bromley players were founder members of the English Bowling Association and the London and Southern Counties Bowling Association. Bromley's secretary founded and was first secretary of Kent County Bowling Association in 1911.

141. St John the Evangelist was built to supply the needs of fast-growing New Bromley, originally as a chapel-of-ease to the parish church. In about 1871 vicar and churchwardens set about finding a ready-built corrugated iron church. They found one on the Isle of Wight for £450, and it was transferred to Bromley for another £224. This was replaced by a stone building in 1880.

142. Sundridge Park station was built in 1878 as a private station for the Sundridge Park estate so, although it was officially named Plaistow, it was known as Mr. Scott's. In 1894 it was opened for public use and renamed. The cream-washed weatherboarding was typical South-Eastern Railway architecture for country stations and happily looks very little different in 1990.

143.   Street cleaning came under the Local Board of Health before Bromley Borough took over in 1903. Some areas were more difficult to keep clean and tidy than others, especially the more industrial parts, or those areas where roads had not been made up. This smart outfit was photographed in 1912; one wonders how the two men and the horse fared in the Great War.

144. Plaistow Green, 1895. This hamlet at the crossroads consisted of a few cottages and the mansions of Plaistow Hall, Plaistow Lodge and Springfield (home of Major Satterthwaite). The road leading left is London Lane, heading for Bromley Hill. Along Plaistow Lane was the then weatherboarded *Crown Inn*, soon to be rebuilt in Victorian splendour in 1897.

145. Plaistow Lodge, better known as Quernmore School for Boys which flourished here for many years from 1896. The mansion itself is late 18th-century. It was bought in 1822 and presented to the financier, Walter Boyd, by a group of grateful clients whose fortunes he had safeguarded by remaining in Paris at the time of the French Revolution.

146. On Springhill Farm in 1883. In 1851 half the men still worked full-time on the land while others, and many women, worked part-time. So did the children who were kept from school to help with hay-making, harvesting, fruit picking, and gathering acorns for winter fodder. Boys scared the crows.

147. St Mary's church, originally a rather stark, unprepossessing building, was consecrated by the Archbishop of Canterbury in September 1863. The increase in the population of the hamlets of Plaistow, Farwig and Hollow Bottom to the north-west of Bromley, largely as a result of tracts of the Plaistow Lodge estate being sold off for residential development, prompted the need for a church in that area.

148. St Mary's after 1914 when it had acquired its present appearance with the addition of two transepts, a chancel, sanctuary, organ chamber, vestry, Narthex entrance and slender spire. Notice how the trees had grown. The effects of the Great War with falling congregations and income prevented its completion, by further additions of two side aisles and a steeple, as planned.

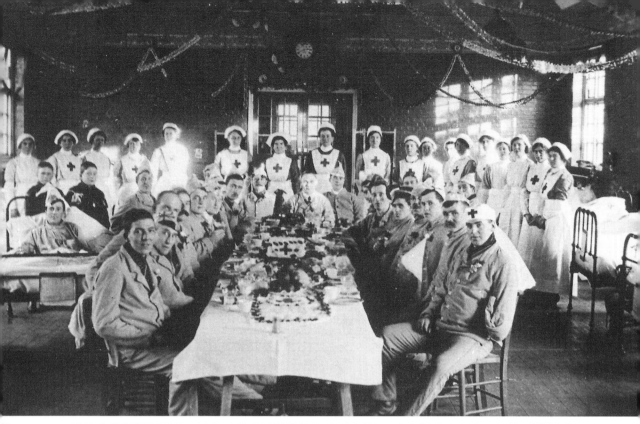

149. St Mary's church hall V.A.D. Hospital. A patient who spent several months there reported: 'what splendid work the ladies of Bromley are doing. The V.A.D.s from commandant downwards are marvellous. Everything is done to make the patients happy and comfortable, nothing is too much trouble, everything is done with a smile. As our Tommies would say, "It was worth getting wounded".'

150. In the grounds of Springhill. 'I have nothing but praise for the nurses and doctors at Bromley, also the public, always very kind to us, especially the ladies who took us for so many splendid rides, and if I have to go out to the Front again I hope I may get what we call "a lucky one" and come back to Bromley.'

151. Farwig Lane Mission was founded by a splinter group from the Methodist church in the High Street in 1881. Beginning in a cottage, two years later a temporary iron structure was its home; this was to be enlarged three times. The summer of 1902 saw the introduction of the Great Tent, followed by Sunday evening services in the Grand Hall.

152. The Central Hall, London Road, succeeded the Farwig Mission in its evangelical work, being opened on 14 April 1905 with much joy and the enthusiasm of immense gatherings at the initial ceremony and subsequent meetings. The Hall had chairs for 1,250 (costing 9s. each), a gallery all round, and there was a schoolroom to accommodate about 400, further classrooms and a kitchen.

153. Missionary Choir. This card was posted to a lady in Billericay on 1 July 1909. The message reads: 'Dear A. – can you fancy us walking down London Road in these costumes on Saturday; last night our musical evening went off splendidly. It began at 7 and over at 11 o'clock. There were nearly 90 in the Choir, and hundreds of folks arrived ... P.S. puzzle find the three Bromley Suffragettes'.

154.   London Road between Farwig Lane and Bromley College developed a community of its own when shops were built on the fringes of College Field. On the west side was Lauriston, home from 1883-96 of Mr. (later Sir) Joseph Wilson Swan. He enjoyed demonstrating his scientific inventions to friends and neighbours, and is best remembered for his incandescent electric light bulb.

155.   Tweedy Road was named after John Newman Tweedy who, until 1888, lived at Widmore House at the other end. This part of the property was sold and laid out in streets of pleasant houses between 1881 and 1891. When the family left in 1904 the house became the first County Girls' School and the municipal offices were erected in its grounds.

156. Bromley County Girls' School. This 1908 photograph shows the headmistress and prefects two years before the move to Nightingale Lane. Uniform dress disguised any difference between fee-paying pupils and the one-third who had won scholarships from Bromley and Orpington council schools: no jewellery was permitted, only a watch. Although some commercial subjects were taught, most girls were expected to maintain secondary school standards.

157.   Christ Church. On a cold May evening in 1886 a small crowd gathered to watch the foundation stone of what would for some time be known as the 'Church in the Wood' being laid. Among them was Samuel Cawston who owned and was developing the grounds and woodland of Bromley Hill House, and with his strong evangelical principles was determined to include a church.

158.   The Children's Church built by Samuel Cawston further down Highland Road soon afterwards for Sunday School, children's services and other religious meetings. The main (upper) hall had a small room at each end used as a vestry and a library above two smaller classrooms, a kitchen and storeroom. Mr. Cawston had the final say on all church matters until his death in 1913.

159. Peace celebrations in July 1919 began with a procession by the Mayor and many local organisations led by banners of the National Federation of Discharged and Demobilised Sailors and Soldiers and their band. At a united service on Martins Hill, Bromley's townspeople joined together to sing the hymns 'Through the night of doubt and sorrow' and 'Now thank we all our God'.

160.   The war memorial. Almost before the war ended in November 1918, Bromley's citizens began writing to the local press with proposals for a permanent memorial to the town's fallen. Eventually it was decided that there should be, as well as the memorial, a fund for children who had lost their fathers and a memorial institute. The memorial was unveiled at a moving ceremony on 22 September 1922.

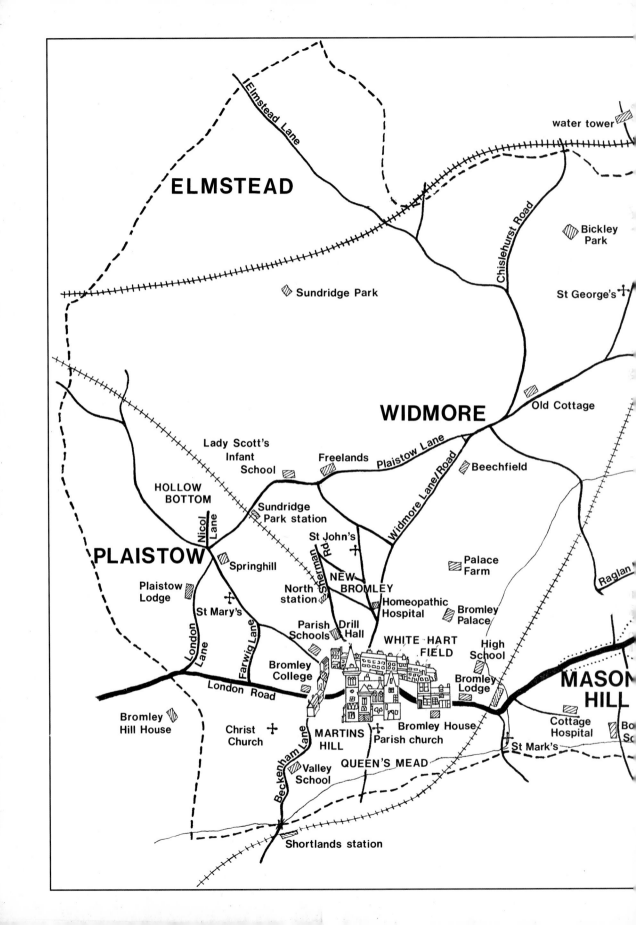